Step-by-Step Emerging Market Investing

A Beginner's Guide to the Best Investments in Emerging Markets

Joseph Hogue

About this Book

Your world is changing.

In 1992, developed countries like the United States and Japan accounted for nearly two-thirds the global economy. By 2015, the percentage of the world economy from these countries has shrunk to less than half while Asia and Latin America have almost doubled their share of the global marketplace.

Public debt of $16.3 trillion in the United States is now larger than the economy and an aging population means economic growth will continue to slow.

The days of parking your money in American companies and enjoying a stable long-term return are over.

Slowing economic growth in the developed world and huge demographic advantages in developing countries are shifting the landscape for corporate profits and stock returns.

Being ahead of these changes means opening your investments to the regions and players that will benefit most over the next several decades. The average American investor holds just 3% of their portfolio in stocks of emerging market countries.

That will leave them dangerously behind the game as the world changes further. Those investing in multi-national U.S. companies as part of their emerging markets investment are in for a surprise. While U.S. companies in the S&P 500 book nearly 40% of their sales overseas, less than half that is from emerging markets.

The fact is that only direct investment in emerging market stocks will provide the growth you need to meet your financial goals and reduce the risk of a stagnant economic picture in the United States and other developed markets.

But emerging market investing is far from a smooth ride to higher returns. Speaking at a Bloomberg conference in 2011, I was one of the few to acknowledge tough years ahead for EM stocks. In fact, the chronic cycle of boom and bust in emerging market stocks means a rebalancing strategy is absolutely essential to keeping your gains.

Step-by-Step Emerging Markets Investing is the only book to give you a detailed process on how to position your investments for the developing change in world markets. You'll get an in-depth review of the risks and upside potential in emerging markets investing as well as the countries and funds in the theme.

The last section of the book is dedicated to a step-by-step process to building your emerging markets portfolio and how to manage your investments in the least amount of time.

In this book you'll learn:

- The seven periods of boom and bust in emerging market investments and what to look for in the future. (pg. 6)
- The three principal risks in emerging markets and warning signs of when to get out! (pg. 15)
- Review of the emerging market regions and 17 countries with tradable stocks (pg. 21)
- How to build a strategy that cuts down on time you spend looking at stocks but still gives your portfolio a chance to outperform (pg. 41)
- How to maintain your emerging markets portfolio and when to sell (pg. 49)

Check out the other three books in the Step-by-Step Investing series to round out your investing strategy. You'll get everything you need to lay out a sleep-at-night investing strategy that will meet your financial goals.

I've put nearly a decade of work as an investment analyst into the series and hope you can use it to develop a simple strategy that will meet your goals. If you find the ideas useful, *please leave a review on Amazon* to let others know.

Joseph Hogue, CFA

Born and raised in Iowa, Joseph Hogue graduated from Iowa State University after serving in the Marine Corps. He worked in corporate finance and real estate before starting a career in investment analysis. Mr. Hogue has appeared on Bloomberg as an expert in emerging market investing and has led a team of equity analysts for sell-side research. His investment analysis has been featured in advisor newsletters, institutional research reports and in the financial press.

He holds the Chartered Financial Analyst (CFA) designation, the gold standard for ethical and professional conduct in investment management.

PeerFinance101.com is a new kind of personal finance blog where readers share their own stories of personal finance challenges and success. There's no one-size-fits-all solution to meeting your financial goals but you'll find a lot of similarities in others' stories and a lot of ideas that will help you get through your own challenges.

Click through to PeerFinance101 for topics from investing to managing debt as well as retirement planning and frugal living.

Step-by-Step Investing: A Beginner's Guide to the Best Investments in Stocks

ISBN-13 (eBook) 978-0-9962321-8-0
ISBN-13 (Print) 978-0-9962321-9-7

Contents

About this Book ii

You're asking the wrong question 3

The Rise of the Emerging Markets 5

Periods of Euphoria and Bust in Emerging Market Investment 6

Risks in Emerging Market Investing 14

General Risks in Emerging Market Investing 15

A World of Upside in Emerging Market Stocks 18

Review of Emerging Market Regions 20

Asia-Pacific 21

Europe, Middle East and Africa (EMEA) 27

Latin America 31

Frontier Markets 37

How to Invest in Emerging Markets 39

Step 1: Creating your Personal Investment Plan 39

Step 2: Building a Core-Satellite Strategy 41

Step 3: Investing in Emerging Market Regions and Countries 43

Step 4: How to Invest in Individual Emerging Market Companies 45

Step 5: Maintaining your Emerging Markets Investments 49

Resources 52

You're asking the wrong question

If there's one question I get most from investors, it's whether now is the right time to invest?

Investors are manic about timing the stock market and trying to profit from the worst advice ever given, buy low and sell high. If there is anything to be learned from the abysmal returns earned by the average investor, it's that market timing just doesn't work.

Instead of asking when to invest, the real question investors should be asking is *where*!

If you picked up this book, I'm guessing you know that the where is in the emerging markets.

Emerging markets have been known by different names over the past several decades. Once called third-world countries, they are also known as newly-industrialized, least-developed and developing nations. There's been just as much disagreement on a definition of qualifications for an emerging market as there have been names but a few characteristics stand out:

- GDP per capita (size of the economy relative to population) is lower than in developed countries
- Institutions like law enforcement and the judicial system do not function as efficiently as those in developed countries
- People may not have access to the technology and capital equipment that is common in developed countries

The World Bank estimates that 86% of the world's population and 75% of its land mass could be classified as emerging. Despite the fact that nearly 6.3 billion people live in emerging market countries, the group only accounts for half of the world's economic wealth and 12% of the global stock market size.

The flip side to this is that the economies of emerging markets are growing much more quickly than that of developed countries like the United States, Japan and the European Union.

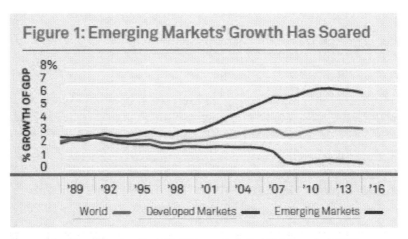

Figure 1: Emerging Markets' Growth Has Soared

Source: International Monetary Fund, World Economic Outlook Database, April 2011.

Economic growth in the emerging world started taking off well before the internet age. Lower wages brought outsourcing jobs from the developed world and spurred industrialization. The web-connected world has only amplified that growth. The internet has allowed education and outsourcing to spread freely and emerging markets are taking full advantage of the opportunity.

Over the last twenty years, this difference in growth between emerging markets and developed economies has shifted the world's economy.

The developed markets accounted for 64% of the world's output in 1992 with emerging Asia and Latin America accounting for just 20% of global output combined. Fast forward to 2015 and the developed world's share of the global economy has shrunk to 47% while emerging Asia and Latin America are more than a third (37%) of total output.

It's not just that economic growth in emerging markets has been increasing. Economic growth in developed markets is slowing as well. Aging populations and slowing population growth means fewer people in the workforce producing fewer goods. The debt burden from public programs and unbridled consumption is detracting from investment in developed economies.

The amount of public debt in Japan and the United States has soared to 230% and 108% of their economies. Compare that with debt-to-GDP ratios of just 37%, 10% and 12% for the emerging economies of China, Chile and Russia.

You don't have to believe the doomsday scenarios of massive default and stagflation for developed markets to understand that the emerging world will have the clear economic advantage over the coming years.

Protecting your wealth and meeting your financial goals means investing in emerging markets.

The Rise of the Emerging Markets

The history of emerging market investing for retail investors has only developed over the last thirty years. The first mutual funds offering emerging market exposure came out in the late 1980s with pioneers like Mark Mobius but it wouldn't be until the early 90s that the market started seeing the potential in EM.

As an economist by training, I was able to see the rise of the emerging markets well before their success started showing through in the stock market. In the mid-1980s, the world was investing in the emerging markets through Foreign Direct Investment (FDI) – investments in businesses and equipment in the region but the emerging markets were not yet investing in the rest of the world. According to the United Nations, the amount of FDI flowing into emerging markets was more than 20% of total global investment but investment flows out of emerging markets into other countries was just 5% of the total.

It's important because it shows how emerging markets were important for foreign businesses looking for growth but that the countries had not really come into their own yet. It wasn't until 2000 that the emerging markets started investing outwards and became bigger players on the international scene.

In the decade to 2010, outflows of investment from emerging markets to other countries grew to about 14% of total global investment. During this period, emerging market businesses were able to make investments in foreign companies and then bring the technology and business processes back home to accelerate growth.

Periods of Euphoria and Bust in Emerging Market Investment

More than perhaps any other theme, investing in emerging markets has been characterized by periods of booming investor sentiment followed by falling prices as near-sighted investors flee the space.

Emerging Markets: Periods of Boom and Bust

Source: Templeton Developing Markets Fund

1991 – 1994

The boom in Japanese economic growth of the '80s and the depth of the 1989 recession in the United States taught investors that there was more to the world than the red, white and blue. Even rebounding economic growth in 1992 was less than average growth booked in the emerging world.

Investors poured into the relatively new option in emerging market funds. Over this first period, the emerging market index jumped 55% against a 22% increase in the S&P 500.

1994 – 1997

A Mexican currency crisis in December 1994 brought emerging market risks back to the forefront. A booming U.S. economy on the tech revolution pushed the value of the dollar higher against the peso which was also struggling due to civil unrest in Mexico. This made it impossible for the country to pay its dollar-denominated debt and the government devalued the currency. A surprise interest rate hike by the Federal Reserve sent many foreign currencies lower on a path to devaluation.

The repercussions flowed through the entire EM space as investors felt the risk was too great, especially against a building tech bubble in the States. Over the period, the emerging market index rose just 23% against a 98% gain in the S&P 500.

1997 – 2003

Another currency crisis in Asia in 1997 and Russia's default on its debt in 1998 led to further losses in emerging market stocks. The emerging market group of stocks rebounded a spectacular 94% in less than a year to December 1999 but was immediately caught in the tech crash in U.S. stocks. The emerging market index lost 51% of its value over the six years to 2003, underperforming an 11% gain in the S&P 500 index.

2003 – 2007

This fourth period marks the rise of emerging markets with strong economic growth in nearly every region. Low interest rates in the United States fueled investment abroad as investors searched for better returns. Economic reform in China produced double-digit growth and the country's demand for raw materials meant huge export revenue to other emerging nations.

Over just four years, the emerging market index zoomed 314% against an 82% gain in the S&P 500.

2007 - 2009

There used to be an old saying in the markets, "When the U.S. sneezes, the rest of the world catches a cold." The idea was that, as the engine of global economic growth, any weakness in the United States translated to recessions and worse in the rest of the world.

At the first sign of economic weakness in the United States, investors have typically fled any risky investments abroad to seek safety in bonds and large U.S. companies. We'll see later that the emerging markets have partially grown beyond this tendency but it hit markets hard in 2007. When the U.S. housing bubble burst, emerging market stocks sank by 71% and underperformed the 52% loss in U.S. stocks.

2009 – 2011

The period following the global financial collapse promised to return emerging market stocks to their prior glory and was really the first time that the group showed it could grow without strong economic growth in the developed world. The group surged 138% over the two years to March 2011, beating returns on the S&P 500 by 58%, on continued growth in China and high commodity prices.

2011 – Present (2015)

From the spring of 2011 to present, several factors have weighed on emerging market stocks. China's fantastic economic growth has started to slow and its demand for raw materials like copper, coal and iron ore has fallen significantly. Tremendous investment in the mining sector over the boom years led to oversupply in many of the industrial metals and prices have plummeted with lower demand and still relatively high supply. This has hit especially hard those countries that didn't use the boom years as an opportunity to diversify their economies away from commodity exports.

The European debt crisis in 2011 and sluggish economic growth in Europe also helped to slow the pace of growth in emerging markets. Besides an uncertain market for emerging country exports, the debt crisis has strengthened the U.S. dollar and driven investors to the safety of U.S. stocks. Since most commodities are priced in dollars, this has only caused prices of metals and energy products to fall further.

2015 and Beyond?

Looking at the history of emerging market investing over the past quarter of a century brings out the biggest risk in the group, that of euphoria and busts.

While buy-and-hold has worked with investing in U.S. stocks, returning an average 7.6% annually since 1991, investors may need to manage their exposure in emerging markets a little closer.

A buy-and-hold investment in the emerging market group of stocks yielded an annual return of 6% over the period above but a system of careful rebalancing each year nearly doubled the returns to 10% annually. We'll talk more about how to rebalance your investments each year to take advantage of the ups and downs in EM stocks.

Naysayers will point to the multiple periods of disappointing returns in emerging market stocks and say that it's not worth the risks. Only looking at the past denies the progress in economic policy and stability that we've seen in the EM group over the last two decades.

While the surging value of the dollar has held back emerging markets over the past year, it hasn't led to the kind of collapse that was chronic in the past. Emerging markets are managing their dollar-denominated debt and building stability funds to smooth out rough periods.

Even as slowing economic growth in China and a sluggish U.S. economy no longer provide the once critical requirement for EM growth, many emerging countries are posting strong economic growth. India and Vietnam booked economic growth of 7.4% and 6.0% in 2014, more than twice the 2.4% GDP growth in the United States.

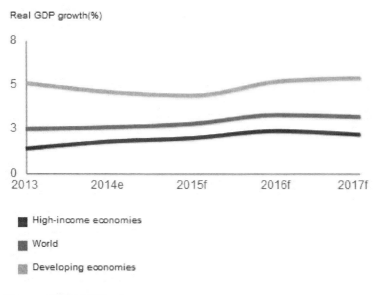

Real GDP growth(%)

- ■ High-income economies
- ■ World
- ■ Developing economies

Source: World Bank

Investor enthusiasm for emerging market stocks may rise and fall but the bigger economic picture is undeniable. Aging populations and debt burdens in developed markets like the U.S., Japan and Europe will mean ever slower economic growth. A younger, growing population and technology will drive economic growth in the emerging world.

Where would you rather invest your money?

There are two principal ways investors get access to emerging market stocks.

American Depositary Receipts

When a foreign company wants to offer shares to U.S. investors, it issues American Depositary Receipts (ADRs). The company then deposits a number of its shares in a holding bank with each ADR representing a certain number of the actual shares. It's an arrangement that works out for both the investor and the foreign company.

By issuing ADRs, foreign companies get access to the U.S. capital markets for financing. Investing in ADRs means U.S. investors can get exposure to foreign companies without having to open an account on a foreign stock market. Investors in ADRs also get the peace of mind knowing that the foreign company is required to register and file financial statements annually on Form 20-F with the Securities & Exchange Commission (SEC).

Since ADRs are traded in dollars, the performance of the shares and the company's shares in the foreign market will vary depending on the change in currencies. When the value of the dollar is falling against other currencies, ADRs tend to do better because foreign assets are worth more in dollar terms. The opposite is true when the dollar rises against other currencies.

Exchange Traded Funds

Exchange traded funds (ETFs) are like mutual funds in that managers buy a collection of investments and sell shares in the whole group to investors. The manager determines which stocks to hold in the fund according to the fund rules and charges investors an annual fee to invest.

While mutual funds are still popular in employer-sponsored plans like 401k programs, ETFs are the better deal for investors.

- Annual fees for ETFs are much lower than those charged on mutual funds, often by 1% or more.
- You only pay taxes on your investment gains in ETFs when you sell the fund whereas you might owe taxes annually on mutual funds whether you sell or not.
- ETFs trade like stocks throughout the day and commissions are low with online trading websites. Mutual fund prices only adjust at the end of each day so you won't know at what price you're buying or selling until the market closes.

There are hundreds of ETFs that offer exposure to emerging market stocks, many of which I highlight in the book. ETFs are a critical part of your overall investing strategy because they give you diversification over a large group of stocks with just one purchase. We'll cover an investing strategy using ETFs along with individual stock picks later on in the book.

Risks in Emerging Market Investing

Investing in emerging market stocks generally involves more risk than buying shares of large American companies or those of companies headquartered in other mature markets. The opportunity and potential for returns far outweighs the risks but I wanted to highlight them within a separate section so there's no doubt.

It's not that I want to scare you by outlining the hazards in emerging market stocks but to give you a better understanding of what the risks are and how they affect stock prices. That way, you can make your own decisions instead of listening to what the near-sighted market is saying.

You see, professional analysts and the investing public are about as manic-depressive as it comes when talking about emerging market stocks. When times are good, they love EM stocks and pitch the upside to no end. When stock prices fall, suddenly the risks are not worth it and no one should invest in the space.

Even though the return on EM stocks has outperformed the S&P 500 over the last 15 years, if you didn't fully understand the risks then you might be convinced by the rest of the market to sell out at exactly the wrong time.

General Risks in Emerging Market Investing

There are a few risks that are inherent to emerging market investing almost by definition. These risks will always be present but you may be able to avoid the worst dangers by understanding the warning signs.

Political risk: Most emerging markets have less stable political regimes when compared to the developed world. This ranges from the constant threat of power shifts and expropriation in some countries to only marginal changes to the tax structure in others.

Much of the political risk in emerging markets can be reduced by watching the international news and following the general trend in political discourse.

- A weakening economy heading into general elections may give rise to a change in power and popular sentiment.
- Follow a scale of economic freedom like the one provided by The Heritage Foundation
- Is the difference in economic wealth between rich and poor increasing or decreasing in the country?

Even at the extreme, political risk may not completely sink your portfolio. For example, Thailand has had two military coups in the last 15 years (2006 and 2014) but the stock market has returned 180% over the period.

Currency risk: Changes in currency values are at the heart of many of the past's biggest collapses in emerging market stocks. From the Mexican peso crisis of 1994 to the Asian crisis of 1997, emerging market investors have been whipsawed by currency movements.

In the past, much of the problem was because emerging markets borrowed and paid their debt in dollars. If the value of their currency fell against the greenback, their debt payments would go up in terms of their money. Rampant inflation has often exacerbated other factors, devaluing foreign currencies against the relative stability of the U.S. dollar.

This problem in currency risk has been reduced by the trend to borrow in local currency debt instead of dollars. Before the 2000s, markets were not confident enough of emerging market growth to extend credit in local currencies. When debt is loaned in the local currency, the payment is fixed in local terms and the debtor doesn't have to worry as much about big currency fluctuations.

Currency risk has also been reduced by inflation targeting by central banks in emerging markets. In the past, monetary authorities would just target a rate of economic growth or would be forced by politicians to print more money to pay for popular programs. This led to runaway inflation and currencies sank against the dollar.

Most central banks now watch both inflation and growth, balancing the two with their policy decisions. It is still a good idea to watch the pace of inflation within the emerging markets in which you invest. Increasing rates of inflation could be a warning sign if they happen for too long or occur too quickly.

Currency risk is still a big factor in emerging markets investing for a couple of reasons. Investing in a foreign company means you have an ownership share of that company's assets and its profits, both denominated in the foreign currency. If the currency weakens or the relative value of the dollar increases, those assets and profits are worth less in dollar terms. If your shares are denominated in dollars, as with ADRs, then the share price will fall.

Changes in currencies also affect economic growth. Many emerging economies are dependent on exports of commodities like oil and metals. Since most commodities are priced in dollars on the international market, a strengthening of the dollar means the price of these commodities decreases. Countries like Venezuela and Russia have suffered greatly because they have been unable to diversify their economies away from a dependency on oil exports.

Despite the currency risk inherent in emerging market investing, the long-term trend is in your favor and there are ways to reduce the risk.

A growing debt burden in the United States and negative population factors could mean the dollar returns to its long-term trend downward against other currencies. This would mean stronger returns on your emerging market investments in dollar-terms.

You can reduce your currency risk by diversifying your investments across different regions and different countries. By owning stocks of companies from many countries and currencies, you reduce your risk in any one particular currency or region.

Correlation risk: The idea of diversification is central to investing and basically just means spreading your total investment across different countries, sectors and different assets like stocks and bonds. The problem is the market's neurotic perspective on emerging markets.

When economic growth slows in one region or political unrest builds, the market has a tendency to sell off all emerging market regions and investments. Investors get scared and throw good investments out with the bad in a race to protect their portfolios.

It's tough to sit there calmly with the conviction of your decision when everyone else is selling and stock prices are falling. This is true in any investment but even more so in emerging markets because the selloff can be even more severe.

One solution is to set a calendar schedule for rebalancing your portfolio. Only buy or sell stocks on a specific date and commit to not trading in and out of the market on news in the meantime.

A World of Upside in Emerging Market Stocks

After studying the risks to emerging market investing, you might be tempted to avoid the group altogether. Don't forget that the market rewards higher risks with higher return.

Besides the potential to higher returns from stronger economic growth, there are other reasons to invest in emerging market stocks.

Emerging market stocks tend to be relatively cheaper than their U.S. counterparts. Over the last decade, stocks in the S&P 500 have traded for an average price of 14.1 times their next year's expected profits. Over the same period, emerging market stocks in the MSCI index have traded for an average price of 11.3 times their next year's expected earnings. Emerging market stocks are (on average) 20% cheaper than U.S. stocks.

Emerging market stocks generally pay higher dividend yields compared to U.S. stocks as well. There are 485 companies in the MSCI Emerging Markets index that pay a dividend yield over 2% a year compared to just 314 U.S. stocks. The iShares MSCI Emerging Markets ETF pays a dividend yield of 2.55% annually compared to a yield of 2.15% for stocks in the S&P 500.

Finally, even though emerging market stocks by themselves are more risky than stocks of U.S. companies, adding them to your portfolio can actually reduce your overall investment risk. It's because emerging market stocks do not rise and fall in unison with stocks in the United States. Different economic cycles and other issues affect the markets differently meaning that stocks in some countries may rise while those in other countries fall. By adding emerging market stocks to your portfolio, you can smooth out your overall investing returns while boosting gains with faster-growing markets.

Review of Emerging Market Regions

Let's take a look at the emerging market regions as well as some of the most accessible countries to foreign investors. Most regions and countries will have exchange traded funds available as well as individual companies through ADRs. There are other ETFs and mutual funds beyond those listed here but many are very thinly-traded so you may have to pay a high price above the going market rate.

Again, it's important to note that you need to watch the percentage you have invested in any particular country when you are picking regional funds. Many ETFs hold a large proportion of the investment in the largest markets like China, Brazil and Russia. You can increase your exposure to other countries by investing in their specific country fund.

The figure shows the proportion of the emerging market index for the largest six countries. I have excluded Korea and Taiwan, which are included in many funds but may not really qualify as EM depending on your definition.

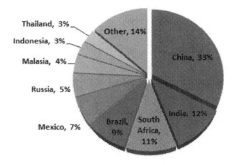

Emerging Markets by Share in Index

- Thailand, 3%
- Indonesia, 3%
- Malasia, 4%
- Russia, 5%
- Mexico, 7%
- Brazil, 9%
- South Africa, 11%
- India, 12%
- China, 33%
- Other, 14%

Source: MSCI EM Index (September 2015)

The slowdown in growth and the political issues in the most popular emerging markets like China, Brazil and Russia have led businesses to look for growth in the smaller countries. While the smaller countries often see their stock markets rise and fall along with China, many are making good progress in developing away from natural resources. You may also want to look to the smaller markets when looking for long-term growth of your portfolio.

Asia-Pacific

The Asia-Pacific region gets the most attention among emerging market investors and is heavily weighted in most global EM funds. The iShares MSCI Emerging Markets ETF holds 70% of its fund in the region's stocks and eight of the 17 countries in which it invests.

South Korea and Taiwan were the first countries in the region to develop and some investors, myself included, no longer include them in the list of emerging markets.

Despite the classification as one region, there are immense differences amongst the countries. More than half the world's population lives within the area and, despite strong economic growth, nearly half that population lives on less than one dollar a day. While population growth will slow to about 0.5% a year through 2030, the sheer size of the region means fast growth in labor markets can drive economic growth compared to the rest of the world.

Besides a strong driver from population growth, the region has historically benefited from relatively free capital markets and open economies. Beyond the obvious exception of China, five of the emerging nations in the region are among the top 30 on The Heritage Foundation's Index of Economic Freedom. Even China with its command economy has moved to market reforms and stability in business practices.

China

Since the late 1990s, you couldn't have a conversation about emerging markets without talking about China. The country's growth and economic size has meant that its demand for raw materials has been the primary factor for success in many resource-exporting markets.

China is something of a mystery when it comes to economic freedom and growth. As a socialist economy, the government technically owns all resources but has allowed a high amount of economic freedom.

Economic growth has slowed with the target of 7% in 2015 to be the lowest since 1990. Despite the slowdown, that pace of economic growth is impressive for the world's second largest economy. There is little doubt that China will be a major economic player in the future and all investors should consider holding some exposure to its market.

India

India's economic growth has been a function of an amazingly-low base and the population's proficiency in English. Despite strong economic growth over the last two decades, GDP is still only $4,077 per capita. The country has been a strong draw of outsourcing though progress in internet access has increased competition among other regional countries.

India's position as a provider of outsourced IT services has helped its service sector to develop, now one of the most developed in the region. Agriculture still accounts for 49% of the workforce but has dropped to 17% of the economy. With a population over 1.2 billion, the trend to urbanization will help India post strong economic growth for years to come.

Despite recent reforms by Prime Minister Modi, the government still has significant control over business through state-owned enterprises and corruption is a constant problem. For this reason, the country ranks poorly on measures of economic freedom. Reforms will be difficult because, like many markets, kickbacks and bribery are an accepted part of the system and considered a part of normal business by many.

Vietnam

Vietnam has followed China's market policies to become one of the fastest growing economies in the region. The country remains a communist dictatorship and is often called out by rights organizations for political repression but has opened its market gradually and joined the World Trade Organization in 2007.

The country has become a top exporter of agricultural products including rice, coffee, shrimp and catfish. A low $4,012 per capita GDP means the country will likely continue to grow in sectors requiring a high amount of labor-intensive work.

Indonesia

The country ranks 22nd among the 41 regional countries in the index of economic freedoms. Corruption in politics and business is a problem, especially in the labor market, but reforms around the 2011 development plan have had some success. President Widodo, elected in 2014, ran on a campaign of economic reform and an end to corruption.

The country is one of the poorer in the region with a GDP of just $5,214 per capita. Indonesia is the world's most populous Muslim democracy.

Malaysia

Malaysia is a success story for the region with a GDP of $17,748 per capita and unemployment lower than many developed countries. It ranks 8th in the region on the economic freedom index on an open economy and the development of a strong business climate.

The government manages several sovereign wealth funds including the Employees Provident Fund, the fourth largest pension fund in Asia.

Petroleum products make up about a quarter of exports but the country also has a strong export capacity in technology products, accounting for a third of the economy.

Philippines

Economic growth in the Philippines has lagged other countries in the region, partly due to the relative role of agriculture in the economy. Agriculture employs nearly a third (32%) of the population but only accounts for 12% the economy. Further urbanization of the population will help the country develop at a faster rate.

The country is making strong progress in economic freedom, ranking 13th within the region, despite lingering political corruption. Much of the population is highly proficient in English and the economy has benefited greatly from outsourcing, likely a key driver of growth to come considering the country's GDP of just $4,682 per capita.

Thailand

Political unrest and conflicts between urban and rural groups have weakened the investment case for Thailand over the last few years. The country has had 19 military coups since becoming a constitutional monarchy in 1932, the most recent in 2014. Public freedoms are routinely restricted but the country still ranks 12th in economic freedom within the region, largely on its prior economic success.

Thailand has a relatively diverse economy with manufacturing supporting 44% of GDP but other sectors like tourism contributing as well. GDP of $9,875 per capita puts it on the higher side of the region.

Regional Funds:

SPDR S&P Emerging Asia Pacific (GMF)

Country ETFs:

iShares MSCI Singapore (EWS)

iShares MSCI South Korea (EWY)

iShares China Large-Cap (FXI)

SPDR S&P China (GXC)

iShares MSCI India (INDA)

India Earnings Fund (EPI)

Market Vectors Vietnam (VNM)

iShares MSCI Indonesia (EIDO)

iShares MSCI Malaysia (EWM)

iShares MSCI Philippines (EPHE)

MSCI Thailand Capped (THD)

Europe, Middle East and Africa (EMEA)

Looking over the region known as EMEA, you get the sense that it is the catch-all for the rest of the emerging market outside of Asia and Latin America. Development in Europe has meant there are not many countries still classified as emerging while most of the countries in Africa are still so undeveloped as to be considered 'frontier' markets. Much of the Middle East is still owned privately and the financial markets are relatively undeveloped.

The region is not well covered in the global emerging market funds.

The iShares MSCI Emerging Markets ETF holds just 15% of its fund in regional stocks with exposure to Russia, South Africa, Turkey and Poland. There are a few regional funds that provide exposure but each typically weights one or two countries heavily.

I have included the region known as the Central and Eastern European countries (CEE) in this group as well because there is some overlap. The CEE region is typically referred to as the countries of Albania, Bulgaria, Croatia, Czech Republic, Hungary, Poland, Romania, Slovenia, Russia and the three Baltic States. Besides the overlap, there really isn't much selection for funds in the CEE region to merit its own section. The regional fund is heavily weighted to Russia (57%), Turkey (17%) and Poland (16%) though it does provide some exposure to Hungary, the Czech Republic and Kazakhstan.

Another fund, the iShares MSCI Emerging Markets EMEA (EEME) provides exposure to the entire region including the CEE countries as well as Africa and the Middle East.

Poland

Poland still makes most lists as an emerging market but I'm not sure I would consider it as such. GDP of $21,214 per capita is still relatively low compared to developed markets but much higher than most emerging countries. Economic growth has slowed considerably over the last decade and future catalysts for growth are limited.

Inefficiency and the productivity gap relative to European counterparts is the most often cited problem for Poland, especially in large sectors like agriculture, manufacturing and mining. Despite its drawbacks, the country's proximity and relationship with Europe should help it to grow at a relatively stable pace and catch up with developed nations in the area.

Russia

Russia is one of the largest emerging markets and a member of the BRICs group of most popular developing markets. Market reforms in the 1990s privatized many of the state-owned companies but the economy remains closely controlled by the government. Subsidies for remaining state-owned companies limit competition and the government reviews foreign investment for approval.

Corruption, labor market issues and increasing controls on monetary freedom puts Russia low on the scale of economic freedom. GDP of $17,884 per capita is higher than most emerging markets though weakness in energy prices has threatened economic growth.

Energy products account for 68% of Russia's exports and half of the government's fiscal revenue. This makes for huge gains when oil prices are rising but has led to recession and massive uncertainty on lower prices. The country's inability to develop outside of energy production has kept it as an emerging nation despite huge resource wealth and a large population.

Because of its dependency on oil revenues, Russia's currency is extremely volatile and has been a source of problems in the past. The country defaulted on its debt in 1998 but now has a sizable economic stabilization fund that should help see it through low oil prices.

Turkey

Turkey is another of the emerging market countries on the cusp of developed nation status. The industrial sector is a significant segment of the economy, especially shipbuilding where the country ranks fourth in the world. GDP per capita of $15,353 is among the highest in the emerging world.

Inflation has chronically been a problem for Turkey with prices rising 7% a year recently and double-digit inflation before 2003. The country's proximity to Syria, Iraq and Iran has meant a constant stream of refugees through the country. Many of the migrants pass through to Europe but geo-political risk is high.

South Africa

South Africa is the only nation in Africa not classified as a frontier market and accounts for 24% of the continent's GDP. While inflation has come down significantly to around 6% a year, unemployment of 20% and higher is still a problem.

Precious metals mining continues to be one of the country's biggest drivers with gold, platinum and diamonds accounting for 28% of total exports. Manufacturing has grown in importance, especially given the relative stability compared to other African nations, and accounts for 15% of the economy.

The persistent employment problem has contributed to the flight of human capital. The government needs to address the problem or the young and educated will continue to leave the country for better opportunities elsewhere. GDP of $11,259 per capita is higher than many Asian countries but still relatively low compared to most of the developing world.

Regional Funds:

iShares MSCI Emerging Markets EMEA (EEME)
SPDR S&P Emerging Middle East & Africa (GAF)
Central Europe, Russia and Turkey ETF (CEE)
iShares MSCI Emerging Markets Eastern Europe (ESR)

Country ETFs:

Market Vectors Russia (RSX)

iShares MSCI Turkey (TUR)

iShares MSCI Poland Capped (EPOL)

iShares MSCI South Africa (EZA)

Latin America

Latin America, the countries from Mexico south to the tip of South America, has been where I have spent most of my professional career in emerging markets analysis. As a trade consultant to Colombian businesses ahead of the Free Trade Agreement with the United States, I got a first-hand look at the region's business climate and the entrepreneurial spirit among its people.

Less popular than the Asia-Pacific region, Latin America is no less an opportunity for emerging market investors. The region benefits from its proximity to the United States for trade and the rise of the consumer class is driving retail business and consumption. Once marked by abject poverty, more than 70 million people were lifted into the middle class through strong economic growth over the ten years to 2010.

The risks for investors in Latin America are primarily from two sources. Despite the growth of the middle class and consumer spending over the past two decades, much of the region's economies still rely on commodity exports like oil, copper and gold. Part of the region's success in the decade to 2010 was linked to high commodity prices and a fast-growing China that needed the raw materials.

The other principal risk in Latin America is political risk, especially in a few key countries. Markets like Brazil, Argentina and Venezuela lie on one end of the spectrum with governments that hold a high level of control over the business sector and are quick to change the rules. On the other end are countries like Chile and Colombia which have fostered an open and stable environment for businesses.

Despite the fact that China's economic growth will probably continue to slow and commodity prices could be weak for a year or more, investing in Latin American stocks still offers great long-term opportunity for investors. Even on a decrease in consumer sales in many countries, the region is still showing strong growth in its middle class. The chart shows retail sales growth in 2014 and over the first three months of 2015. By comparison, retail sales growth in the United States and Europe is generally between just 1% and 2.5% a year.

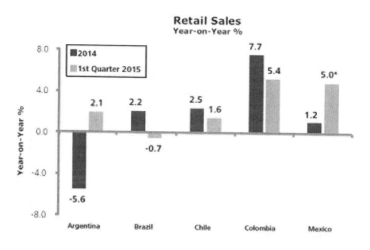

Retail Sales
Year-on-Year %

Source: CAME and statistical institutes in each country

Financial services and access to banking is also helping to develop the region. Over the four years to 2014, more than 67 million adults opened a bank account to bring financial access to 237 million people in the region according to the World Bank's Global Findex survey. Still, only about two-thirds of adults in the region have a bank account and only 42% carry a credit card.

As consumer spending continues to grow, the market for financial services will grow and help to drive faster economic growth. This will help move the region's economies away from commodities and investors will enjoy a more stable trend in returns.

The chronic problem of political risk is a bigger issue for some countries. While Brazil and Argentina offer persuasive growth over brief periods, poor management of the economy can wipe out years of returns quickly. Investors may want to hold more exposure to countries that have proven to be more politically and economically stable like Chile, Colombia, Mexico and Peru.

The region is not well covered by global emerging market funds. The iShares MSCI Emerging Markets ETF holds just 12% of its fund in regional stocks with exposure to Brazil, Mexico and Chile.

Argentina

Argentina's population of 41 million has historically enjoyed one of the most developed economies in the region with spending power of $18,750 per capita. Unfortunately, poor management by several governments have plunged the country into economic repression. The country defaulted on its foreign debt in 2001 and refused to make debt payments in 2014, leading to a technical default. The Heritage Foundation places the country third to last on its scale of economic freedom, just above Venezuela and Cuba.

There is hope on the horizon for investors. Elections in late 2015 could usher in a new age of better economic decisions. Agriculture accounts for 54% of total exports so the country isn't as dependent on energy prices as others in the region.

Brazil

Brazil is a massive exporter of agriculture, industrial materials and energy products. Agricultural products like soybeans and sugar account for a fifth of exports while iron ore and petroleum each account for about ten percent of exports.

While Brazil is the largest economy in the region and one of the most popular with investors, corruption and poor management within the government have wasted much of the opportunity. The country ranks 21st of 29 on the Heritage Foundation index and massive protests have broken out over the last several years.

Brazil won the rights to the 2014 FIFA World Cup and the 2016 Summer Olympics. Public discontent on spending for the two events has tested the government's popular support but presidential elections will not be held again until 2018.

Chile

Chile has long been the model of economic growth for Latin America. It ranks as the most economically free country and sports $19,067 GDP per capita.

Copper accounts for 50% of the country's exports and recent weakness in prices has slowed economic growth. China has slowed its buying considerably and global supply of copper exceeds demand. Fiscal responsibility led Chile to establish a resource stabilization fund in 2007 to smooth its economic dependence on commodity prices. In September 2015, the fund had a market value of $15 billion or about 4.4% of the country's GDP.

Chile's history of economic openness and fiscal strength should help it endure weak copper prices and drive growth in the future.

Colombia

Colombia has benefited from decades of political stability and a business-friendly climate. Since 2011, the country signed free trade agreements with Canada, the United States and the European Union. Despite strong economic growth, the country is still one of the poorest of tradable countries in the region with a GDP of $11,189 per capita.

Colombia's ranking on the Heritage Foundation Economic Freedom index only trails Chile in the region. Nearly 40% of the country's exports are tied to energy products, mostly oil and coal, so any weakness in energy commodities will affect stock prices and the larger economy. A favorable business climate helps the country to attract foreign investment from other countries and should drive economic development in the future.

Peru

Though Peru has historically been further to the socialist side of the political spectrum, the country has benefited from market reforms since the 1990s. Free trade agreements have increased economic activity and the country ranks 8th on the index of economic freedom in the region.

Mining accounts for a large portion of the economy with exports of gold and copper adding to 38% of total exports. Dependence on metal mining and a populist government often make for risk to changes in resource taxes and worker strikes are common.

Mexico

Mexico's trade relationship with the United States has always shielded it from many of the problems seen in other Latin American countries. As a slowing China drags the rest of the region down, Mexico has benefited from relatively strong economic growth to the north.

Market reforms by President Nieto, elected in 2012, have helped to open up key markets like energy and telecommunications. The pace of change is slower than many would have liked but should help to boost competition and open the markets to foreign companies.

Corruption in business and public services is still a problem but the country still ranks highly on the economic freedom index.

Regional Funds:

iShares Latin America 40 (ILF)

Country ETFs:

iShares MSCI Brazil Capped (EWZ)

iShares MSCI Mexico Capped (EWW)

iShares MSCI Chile Capped (ECH)

InterBolsa FTSE Colombia 20 (GXG)

iShares MSCI All Peru Capped (EPU)

FTSE Argentina 20 (ARGT)

Frontier Markets

Frontier markets are those countries that have not quite achieved emerging market status in their economic size but are growing rapidly. The risks are extremely high due to lack of political freedoms, economic policies and openness to foreign markets but these markets may also offer some of the best returns over a long-term investing period.

Besides countries that have yet to become emerging markets, i.e. Jamaica, Bulgaria, Lithuania, Nigeria, Jordan, Saudi Arabia and Pakistan, often an emerging country will be reclassified as frontier because of economic failure or a loss of economic freedoms. After its default in 2014, many believe that Argentina should no longer be considered as an emerging nation.

Many of the frontier markets are relatively closed to foreign investment and few companies trade as ADRs in foreign markets. A couple of ETFs offer the opportunity to invest in the local market or hold shares in foreign-listed companies.

Regional Funds:

MSCI Frontier 100 Index (FM)
Guggenheim Frontier Markets (FRN)

How to Invest in Emerging Markets

As we have done in the other step-by-step books in the series, any process of putting together an investing strategy must start with your own financial needs and tolerance for risk. It's something most investors neglect, skipping over to go directly to picking stocks, but is absolutely critical to your success in investing.

Step 1: Creating your Personal Investment Plan

We went into detail on how to make your personal investment plan and how to determine your risk tolerance in Step-by-Step Investing but will cover the basics here.

Your personal investment plan starts with understanding how much money you'll need to reach your financial goals. This includes spending on education, vacations, large planned purchases as well as normal expenses during retirement. You don't need to be precise down to the penny, especially if you've got more than a decade or two to retirement, but you should have a general idea of how much you'll need to live comfortably.

While it may be an oversimplification, the general rule of withdrawing 4% of your investments to pay for expenses is a good start. This means that the starting value of your investments when you retire should be about 25 times your planned annual expenses. You can probably get away with a portfolio 20 times your expenses since living expenses, other than medical, tend to fall quickly as you get older.

Once you know how much you need in retirement, you can start to play around with financial calculators on the internet to see how much you need to save and what kind of a return you need each year.

Warning: If you find that you need an annual return over 8% every year to retirement to meet your financial goals, something needs changed in your plan. A return higher than about 8% on a diversified portfolio of stocks, bonds and real estate is just not realistic. A lot of investors find they need returns of 10% or higher a year and put all their money in the riskiest stocks. They end up getting beaten and battered by stock market crashes and never end up meeting their goals.

Instead of unrealistically chasing return, reassess how much you can save each month or lower the amount you need for retirement.

You also need to understand your risk tolerance for investments. It does no good investing in high-risk, high-return stocks if you lose sleep and panic-sell whenever the market takes a tumble.

There are risk tolerance questionnaires on the internet but finding your comfort with risk is pretty easy.

1) How many years do you have until you need to depend on the money? If you have more than ten years to invest, you'll have more time to take advantage of higher returns in stocks without worrying about a stock market selloff. If you have less than ten years, you can't afford to take a big hit because you might not have time to recover.

2) When you see the stock market and your investments fall rapidly, does it cause you to lose sleep? If you're uncomfortable with big changes in wealth, you'll want to put more money in safer investments.

3) What kind of investments do you usually prefer? Do you go for the high-flying, risky investments or do you generally prefer the slow-and-steady approach? There's nothing wrong with taking a little more risk if that's what you like but understand your comfort level before you invest.

4) How stable is your income? You can take a little more investment risk if your income is more certain. Tenured professors have an almost guaranteed income so they can take more investment risk. People that work in the financial markets might take less investment risk because their income can rise or fall quickly depending on the economy.

Knowing your risk tolerance will first help decide how much of your money to put in asset classes like stocks, bonds and real estate. It will also help decide how to invest within each asset class as well. While you will always want some stocks in your portfolio, you may want to limit the amount you have in riskier stocks or groups like emerging markets as your risk tolerance decreases.

While your own risk tolerance will determine how much of your total stock portfolio you invest in emerging market stocks, you probably should limit it to no more than 25% and no less than 5% of the amount in stocks. Besides the money you directly invest in EM stocks, you'll also get some exposure through stocks of large companies that book sales overseas.

Step 2: Building a Core-Satellite Strategy

The core-satellite strategy is a great way to build your investments in general but especially relevant for emerging market investing.

A core-satellite strategy means investing the majority of your money (the 65% to 80% core) in broad funds and the rest of your money around individual stocks.

For example, within your emerging markets portfolio, you might invest the majority of your money in the Vanguard Emerging Markets ETF (VWO) which holds more than 1,000 stocks across 21 different emerging countries. This would give you broad exposure to the whole emerging markets theme and potential return.

For the remainder of your EM portfolio, you might invest in a couple of individual country funds to get extra exposure to growth in that country or you might pick a few stocks of individual companies. From this 'satellite' portion of your portfolio, you are hoping to add a little higher return from countries or companies that you like best.

Example Core-Satellite Emerging Markets Proportions

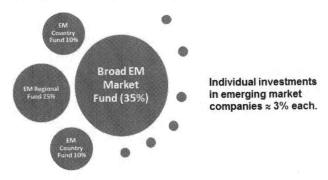

By only investing a small portion of your portfolio in a few individual countries or companies, you cut down on the amount of research and analysis you need to do as well as the amount of time it takes to monitor your stocks for changes. The 'core' portion of your portfolio is a buy-and-hold investment that requires no monitoring while you may need to watch for political changes or economic problems in your individual 'satellite' investments.

You can use the core-satellite approach in your overall portfolio of stocks as well. Your 'core' positions may be broad index funds like the SPDR S&P 500 ETF (SPY) and the Vanguard Total International Stock ETF (VXUS). Around that core, you might hold smaller portions of your stock portfolio in different sectors, emerging markets or small-cap stocks.

The most popular emerging market funds are those that cover the entire theme, funds that invest across all regions. The iShares MSCI Emerging Markets ETF (EEM) and the Vanguard Emerging Markets ETF alone see more than 90 million shares traded every day.

While these general funds will give you broad exposure, the also hold a very concentrated exposure in just a few emerging market countries. For example, the MSCI fund holds 52% of all its investments in just China (24%), South Korea (16%) and Taiwan (12%). Besides the fact that this means more than half of your investment is focused in one region, there is a debate whether South Korea and Taiwan should even be considered emerging markets.

You can still build a core of emerging market investments without using these funds by investing in the regional or country funds. You can invest equal amounts in the regional funds or can weight your investment by factors like relative percentage of the global economy in each region.

Step 3: Investing in Emerging Market Regions and Countries

The way you look for opportunities in emerging market regions and individual countries is the same way you'll watch for any risks in your portfolio. Since companies in emerging markets are much more dependent on the political and economic picture for their success this is really where you need to start in your analysis.

This focus on the political structure and the larger economic theme is called top-down analysis. The idea is to invest in the companies that will have the strong impetus of a healthy economy and political environment behind them.

Reading through the regional review, you'll notice I watch The Heritage Foundation's scale of economic freedom. It isn't the only measure of economic stability but is a good one to follow. You don't need to follow the political or economic situation across all emerging markets, only in those regions and countries in which you invest more heavily than others.

Emerging markets can tend to get volatile up to a year before presidential elections. If the incumbent administration has done a fairly good job and the economy has been growing modestly, there's usually nothing to worry about. Government mismanagement and a weakening economy could lead to civil unrest and a change in political groups in power could change the argument for investing in the country.

An important measure in the economy to watch is the nation's **current account**. The current account is the difference between a country's savings, foreign trade and investments. It is made up of the trade balance (the money received from exports minus the money spent on imports), investment from other countries and to other countries, and other transfers. You don't need to follow each one to understand the bigger picture.

Since most emerging markets are large exporters and do not have developed consumer markets, they should be able to maintain a current account surplus. This means the country will grow richer through exports and investment, eventually leading to development of a more stable consumer market and institutions.

While **inflation** has come under control in many emerging markets with explicit targeting by central banks, it is still something you will need to watch. High inflation will weaken a country's currency and can lead to social unrest due to runaway prices. It isn't necessarily the level of inflation that should worry you but the trend.

Even inflation of up to five or six percent can be manageable if it is consistent every year. If the rate of inflation is increasing every quarter and every year, it might not be long before the government loses control of the situation. The central bank may need to raise rates to slow economic growth and rising prices.

One last economic measure to follow is the amount of dollar-denominated debt by a particular country or company. Since interest rates are typically much lower in the United States, many foreign companies borrow in dollars to reduce the rate they have to pay on debt.

This is fine when economies are growing and foreign currencies are stable but has led to problems when foreign currencies tumble on weak economic conditions. The Bank of International Settlements tracks foreign borrowing of dollar-denominated debt and companies report it on their financial statements.

It may seem like a lot of economics and analysis to get into but it's really only to make an initial strategy and pick a few countries on which to focus. After setting up your strategy, you'll only need to watch for developments in the specific countries or regions in which you invest most heavily.

Step 4: How to Invest in Individual Emerging Market Companies

Finding individual emerging market stocks available as ADRs can be done through the J.P. Morgan ADR search. The ADR search tool lets you filter your search by region, country, exchange on which the stock is listed and by sector.

For U.S. investors, you will want to limit your search to those ADRs traded on the Nasdaq and New York Stock Exchange (NYSE).

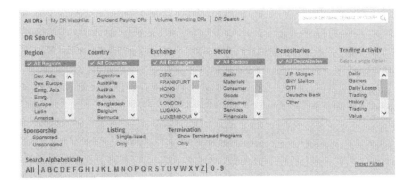

For individual companies, I like to start with my top-down analysis. In contrast to the United States, where companies can do well despite most government policies and changes, it is very difficult for even the best emerging market company to do well in a country with poor government policies and weakening economic fundamentals.

After finding a few countries or regions with improving economies and relatively stable governance, you can narrow your search down to individual companies.

To research individual companies, Morningstar is a good resource for looking at trends in financials. You don't need to be a full-time financial analyst but just look at the trend in revenue (sales) and a few of the other accounts. Are sales increasing over the last few years? Has profitability (margins) increased over the last few years?

Make sure you compare the financial trends against competitors in the same industry. A company with flat or barely-growing sales may still be a strong investment if it competing in an industry where everyone else has had declining sales.

Some basic financials to study:

- **Revenue or sales:** The company should have a general trend higher in sales each year or not have any unexplained drops.
- **Gross margin:** This is the gross profit divided by total sales and is the profitability after taking out the cost of materials.
- **Operating margin:** This is the operating income divided by total sales and is the profitability after taking out business costs. This is an excellent measure to compare across companies within the same industry. Who is the most profitable? If they've been the most profitable for a long time, the company may have a strong competitive advantage.
- **Cash flow from operations:** This is on the statement of cash flows and shows actual business cash flow for the company. Management can manipulate earnings pretty easily but it is harder to fudge the numbers when it comes to cash flow.

You'll also want to compare some basic valuation measures across companies. The **price-to-earnings** (P/E) ratio is the most commonly used and is simply the stock price divided by the company's earnings over the last year. You'll find a lot of the most important measures if you go to Yahoo Finance, then to an individual stock's page and click on Key Statistics in the left-hand menu.

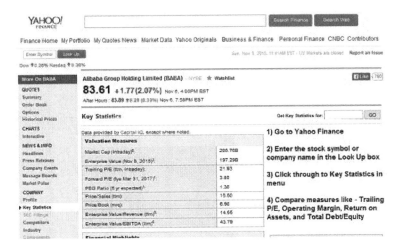

Finally, read through a few analyst reports on the company. You can find these on Morningstar or most online investing sites will provide them if you have an account. Don't take these reports or recommendations as gospel, always do your own analysis as well, but they can help you spot any signs of trouble or bigger issues.

Don't feel like you need to become an expert at stocks. The idea here is to just find a few companies that you really like and can invest in for the next ten or twenty years. You really don't need more than about 20 individual companies in your entire stock portfolio so three to five emerging market companies would be more than enough.

Remember, the idea is to have most of your money in broad ETFs that give you exposure to the larger emerging market theme. Supplementing you core investments with a few individual stocks gives you the chance to see a little higher return on separate companies but still keeps your company-specific risk low and minimizes fees.

Step 5: Maintaining your Emerging Markets Investments

Maintaining your emerging market portfolio will be a little more intensive than maintaining the rest of your stocks.

For your investments in stocks of U.S. and other developed market companies, you don't have to worry much about political risks and larger economic issues. The economies in these countries will go through cycles but recessions generally only last a year or two and the stock market usually rebounds within a few years. You'll rebalance your stocks every year, possibly reducing your exposure in companies that have zoomed higher to put money to funds and companies that have not performed as well.

For your emerging market stocks, you'll need to keep a closer eye on the political risks and some economic measures.

We've actually covered the risks and measures you'll want to follow in the section on setting up you emerging markets strategy. The same measures like economic freedom, political risks, current account and inflation are all things you need to check on every six months to maintain your portfolio.

These measures are all multi-year ideas so don't think you need to check your stocks daily or even monthly. Every six months, note the most current data from an economic freedom scale as well as any developments in other measures. A negative development in any given year may not be anything to worry about nor would a negative trend in just one measure. Only when more than one measure shows a negative trend over a period of years is there a reason to revisit your investments in a particular country or region.

This all should not affect your investment in the broader emerging market funds, those covering the entire theme or possibly even the regional funds. It should only affect your decision to invest in individual countries and companies.

As for your general maintenance strategy, I like waiting six months between buying new investments with excess cash. You should continue to deposit money into your investment account each month but waiting to invest every six months will help to keep your fees lower.

Waiting six months to invest can also help reduce fees around your annual rebalancing. You aren't necessarily investing in new stocks every six months but can use the opportunity to buy more of those investments that have underperformed and less of those that have done well.

Every year or two, you may need to sell some stocks to move money to another asset class like bonds or real estate if your stocks have done really well. This will keep your investment in stocks, bonds and real estate closer to the proportions appropriate for your level of risk tolerance. Every decade, you'll want to revisit your personal investment plan and risk tolerance. As you get closer to retirement, you will want to decrease the amount you invest in stocks while increasing the amount you invest in safer bonds and real estate. This rebalancing will work within your stocks as well, decreasing the amount in riskier stocks while putting more money to safer sectors like utilities and consumer staples.

As with all stocks, the best thing you can do in emerging markets investing is to relax and not get sucked into the regular ups and downs of the market. It helps to understand that you really haven't lost or gained any money, other than the regular dividends you'll receive, until you sell an investment. Since your investments are for very long-term goals, you will hold your stocks for decades and don't need to worry about your returns in any given year.

A Special Request

I hope you've enjoyed Step-by-Step Emerging Markets Investing and found the advice to be helpful in putting together your investing strategy. Throughout the book, I've tried to emphasize the benefit to a simple and basic strategy that meets YOUR financial goals. There's no lack of ways to complicate your investing strategy but the simplest approach will get you to where you want to be with the least amount of headache and sleepless nights.

I'd like to ask one favor as you finish reading the book. Reader reviews are extremely important to the success of a book on Amazon. Reviews play a big part in determining the rank of a book and how many people see it when searching.

If you found the book to be helpful, would you please leave a review on the Amazon page?

It's really easy to do and does not have to be a long, detailed review.

Please click here to leave a review on Amazon

- Just go to the book's page on Amazon (or through the link above) and click on "customer reviews" or scroll down and click on "Write a customer review"
- Your review can be as short as a sentence or as long as you like. Just try describing what you liked about the book and any particular points from a chapter.

I always appreciate honest reviews. Thank you so much!

Resources

Round out your investing plan with the best investments in dividends, emerging markets and bonds. Check out the other three books in the Step-by-Step series:

Learn the secret to building an investing strategy that will meet YOUR needs. The first book in the series covers 10 basic rules of investing you must remember to avoid losing money. You'll get the secret to winning the stock market game as well as a step-by-step strategy for buying stocks. *Click here to buy Step-by-Step Investing.*

Learn the secret to bond investing and how to balance your investments with safety. This book covers how to buy bonds and a simple strategy that will provide a stable income stream you can live on. *Click here to buy Step-by-Step Bond Investing.*

Learn how to put dividend stocks in your portfolio and money in your pocket! This book covers income investments like REITs, MLPs and dividend stocks that have provided strong returns and a regular cash return. ***Click here to buy Step-by-Step Dividend Investing.***

See through the BS and scams in passive income strategies to start building a real source of income today in blogging, real estate, stocks and bonds.

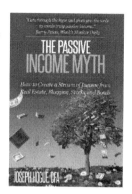

NO fluff, NO theories, and NO sugar coating – just the detailed process on how I put together an income from four sources and make money whether I work or not. *Click here to buy The Passive Income Myth.*

News and Professional Organizations

Check out these websites for news and detailed data on the income investments covered in this book.

Bloomberg – Business and finance news resource that keeps it objective. You'll see some analyst commentary but the ideas are usually fairly balanced.

Morningstar – Professional source of data and company financial information. There is a lot of analysis and advice on the site. Most of it is objective and helpful but avoid using it to make short-term investment decisions.

JP Morgan ADR Search – Tool for finding American Depository Receipts of foreign companies listed on the U.S. exchanges.

Yahoo Finance – An excellent resource for stock information including charts, data and headlines.

Investing and Personal Finance Blogs

Check out these blogs for more advice on personal finance and meeting your long-term goals. Blogs here were chosen for their rational and measured perspective, favoring a long-term approach instead of get-rich-quick schemes.

PeerFinance101 – My blog on personal finance and achieving financial freedom. Financial freedom isn't about getting rich but getting the life you want and making money decisions around that goal. Share your own stories of financial success or learn from others stories.

Side Hustle Nation – A community of part-time entrepreneurs earning financial independence through small business. It's a great resource for finding your passion and turning your hobby into a money-maker.

Barbara Friedberg Personal Finance – Barbara worked as an investment portfolio manager before launching her blog, offering advice following many of the tenets in this book. It's a great site focused on investing and building wealth.

Club Thrifty – Holly and Greg were able to ditch their 9-to-5 jobs after learning to manage their money. The blog focuses on ways to spend smartly, cut debt and earn extra income.

Bible Money Matters – Peter hits all the topics in personal finance but he also talks about faith and family. It's a great blog that will help you lead an inspired life.